Living the Unhindered Life

DR. CLARICE FLUITT

Living the Unhindered Life © 2015 Clarice Fluitt

Unless otherwise noted, Scripture quotations are from the King James Version of the Bible (Public Domain). In some instances they are author's paraphrases.
Scripture quotations marked (AMP) taken from the Amplified® Bible, Copyright © 1954, 1958, 1962, 1964, 1965, 1987 by The Lockman Foundation. Used by permission. (www.Lockman.org)
Scripture quotation marked (NKJV) taken from the New King James Version®. Copyright © 1982 by Thomas Nelson, Inc. Used by permission. All rights reserved.

ISBN: 978-0-9903694-6-2

Publisher: Clarice Fluitt Enterprises, LLC
P O Box 15111
Monroe, LA 71207
www.claricefluitt.com

Acknowledgments

Maya Angelou speaks of gifts this way, "One must know not just how to accept a gift, but with what grace to share it."

I extend my first thanks to the Giver of the gift of life. Without His obedience in the sharing of His life with us, we would have no idea what an unhindered life should look like, nor would we know how to participate in it. I extend my second, third, and fourth thanks to my Executive Assistant, Dr. Tandie Mazule, my Administrative Assistant, Dr. Evon Peet, and my interior designer, Carol Martinez, without whose corporate brilliance, insight, planning, and perseverance this book would not have been written and made available to all who dare to peer into the innermost depths of understanding the way toward Living the Unhindered Life so that they, in turn, can pass the gift forward.

Endorsement

This is an amazing book! There are few workbooks out there as thorough, deep, inspiring, and liberating as Living the Unhindered Life by Dr. Clarice Fluitt. It will empower you to become free from every hindrance you face and will transform your thinking and your life. Each page, story, Scripture and thought provoking question will plant God's word so deep in your heart that you will truly experience a transformed life of freedom and victory. I encourage you to incorporate this book as part of your daily devotions and time with the Lord. Get ready to experience the life God created you to have.

Matt Sorger
Prophetic Healing Minister,
Author and Host of TV's Power for Life

Table of Contents

Foreword

The heart of God is so extravagant! Think about this for a moment: If God gave you His only Son, will He hold anything back from you at all? Nothing is greater than the Son and yet He has given you everything that is within the Son and everything that pertains to Him. He has given you everything!

When an individual gives their life to Jesus Christ, they are born again into the Father's Kingdom. Jesus said, "Fear not, little flock, for your Father has chosen gladly to give you His Kingdom." (Luke 12:32) This is amazing. You have been given His Kingdom.

Many believers following conversion feel unworthy of God's love, promises, and blessings and as a result lean to their own understanding rather than to His truth. They become sin conscious rather than righteousness conscious. They allow the enemy, "the accuser," to bring back to their minds weaknesses and sins of the past even though they have been washed away in God's love through the blood of Christ. When they focus on those lies, they empower them. When they believe the lies, they are caught in a hellish prison of condemnation, guilt, and shame.

Jesus taught, "You shall know the truth, and the truth shall set you free." (John 8:32) The Scriptures also disclose, "As a man thinks in his heart, so is he." (Proverbs 23:7)

It is vital to believe the truth in order to live an unhindered life, and one of the most important foundational truths of the new covenant is that YOU are the righteousness of God in Christ Jesus when you invite Him into your heart to be your Savior.

Dr. Clarice Fluitt's manual, "Living the Unhindered Life," is truly life-giving. The truth contained within will establish you in the righteousness of Jesus Christ. Not righteousness that you produce through dead works, but the gift of righteousness that God gives to everyone who believes.

This manual does not only contain valuable information but it is full of coaching, mentoring, and activation that will establish you in God's gift of righteousness. Oh, it is a glorious book that has the potential to indeed transform your life.

This one revelation of righteousness can change you forever.

Enjoy every line, every verse, every activation and watch yourself arise into the fullness of all that God has created you for. I once heard Dr. Bill Johnson state that Isaiah 60:1 says, "Arise and shine." It does not say, "Arise and reflect." This righteousness is within you. Receive and then let it shine in and through every area of your life. You will find yourself living the "unhindered life."

Patricia King
Founder XP Ministries
Co-Founder XPmedia.com, Inc.

Introduction

Blessed are those who hunger and thirst for righteousness, For they shall be filled. –Matthew 5:6

But to him who does not work but believes on Him who justifies the ungodly, his faith is accounted for righteousness, just as David also describes the blessedness of the man to whom God imputes righteousness apart from works. –Romans 4: 5

Doesn't that just knock a hole in religion? You think, "Wait a minute. Are you telling me that I don't have to do anything?" Exactly. I'm telling you, you only have to believe. This is my refrigerator Scripture. It says that the faith of the person who does not work but believes on Jesus who justifies the ungodly is accounted for righteousness.

Now may He who supplies seed to the sower, and bread for food, supply and multiply the seed you have sown and increase the fruits of your righteousness. –2 Corinthians 9:10

All have sinned and come short of the Glory of God. No one other than Jesus has ever been able to fulfill this Scripture. God is perfect and only perfection can come into His presence. Total obedience, righteousness, and perfection are the same thing before the Lord. When you trust Jesus as your redeemer, you are given an "enter in free" pass. You are entering the presence of God by standing in the place of Christ. Jesus has made you obedient, perfect, and righteous and called you to rule and reign as ambassadors with God forever!

As we begin this study, I pray that there will be not only a listening, but a hearing of the Word of God. Acts chapter 3:18-24 says that Jesus must remain in heaven until the times of the restoration of all things. Restoration means to make things better than they were originally.

Hebrews 9:1-28 tells us that the tabernacle in the Old Testament as well as the system of sacrifices and offerings could never be made perfect nor could it cleanse the consciousness of the people who practiced all of the rituals and ordinances. It could not make it perfect, but we find ourselves living in the process of change and reformation in the body of Christ. As we come to an understanding that the power of all sin is in the law, I ask God to help us understand the gift of righteousness.

The Bible says in Exodus 25:9, *According to all that I show you, that is, the pattern of the tabernacle and the pattern of all its furnishings, just so you shall make it.*

We see in the pattern of the Old Testament that every year the high priest would make atonement for sin, but that atonement was only temporary. Then Jesus, the great high priest, the God man, came and became the absolute sin offering. God said, 'Missing the mark is not part of My plan. When I look at you, I have to see you totally righteous. I cannot see you as a sinner. I cannot see you as a failure.' We are learning through the Word of God that righteousness is a gift which means right standing with God.

In the Old Testament, the law was perfect, but it could not produce perfection. We see that Jesus came with an incredible message. He came teaching about the kingdom of God. He left talking about the kingdom of God. He said in Romans 14:17, *The kingdom of God is not eating and drinking, but righteousness, peace, and joy in the Holy Spirit.*

A few years ago I received this message of righteousness and had to try it in my own life. You see, the only thing you can give away is what you have. If I give it to you and it is not mine, I stole it; but if it becomes mine, if it is revelatory to me, then I can impart it into your spirit. I began to realize that we are made out of dirt, and dirt will grow whatever you plant into it. I began to say, "I've been poor. I've been down and out, beat up and bludgeoned, oppressed, lonely, and hurt," and thought that was the way it was supposed to be.

I was carrying my burden up the hill. I was a sin-conscious person. I kept trying to do, so I could get what I already had by faith, and in so doing kept frustrating the grace of God. I had a form of godliness, but no power that was real. I could pray for other people, but I could not believe for me. I could believe for you all day long. I could get you a house, a car, or a job. I could get your kids saved, healed, and out of drugs, but I was batting zero on my own home front because I was tied up in my own human righteousness instead of understanding that it was a gift God had given to me.

The thing that is keeping us from growing is living with condemnation. We keep trying to 'do' self-righteousness instead of allowing the impartation, the gift, the inheritance of the righteousness of God to prevail. I just had to stand up, appropriate it to myself, and understand that my inheritance is based on the blood of Jesus.

Righteousness must come through faith and not through effort or merit.

And that you put on the new man which was created according to God, in true righteousness and holiness. –Ephesians 4:24

Being filled with the fruits of righteousness which are by Jesus Christ, to the glory and the praise of God. – Philippians 1:11

And be found in Him, not having my own righteousness, which is from the law, but that which is through faith in Christ, the righteousness which is from God by faith. –Philippians 3:9

Your throne, O God, is forever and ever; a scepter of righteousness is the scepter of Your kingdom. –Hebrews 1:8

The purpose of a scepter is to make a decision. The scepter of righteousness is in your hand. Make the decision that you are righteous and qualified.

If you know that he is righteous, you know that everyone who practices righteousness is born of Him. –1 John 2:29

Little children, let no one deceive you. He who practices righteousness is righteous, just as He is righteous. –1 John 3:7

For you, O Lord, will bless the righteous. With favor you will surround him as with a shield. –Psalm 5:12

But the salvation of the righteous is from the Lord; He is their strength in the time of trouble. –Psalm 37:39

Cast your burden on the Lord, and He shall sustain you; He shall never permit the righteous to be moved. –Psalm 55:22

*The righteous shall flourish like a palm tree, He shall
grow like a cedar in Lebanon. –Psalm 92:12*

The word of God and where you are going to flourish
and prosper are all activated when you believe.

My prayer is for my words to have the power to reach
down and unlock in the depths of your heart the
understanding that you never again need to identify with
sin consciousness.

May God bless and enlighten you as you listen to the
CDs and then discipline yourself to carefully read and
answer all the workbook questions.

The things of God become ours by the reason of use.

The Promises of God Legally Belong to the Righteous - NOW!

In this Manual we will learn from the Word of God that everything that is available to Jesus, the Son of God, is available by faith to the redeemed. No longer should we try to become what God's Word says we already are! The Bible teaches that the promises of God legally belong to the righteous —NOW!

> *What shall we say then? That Gentiles, who did not pursue righteousness, have attained to righteousness, even the righteousness of faith; but Israel, pursuing the law of righteousness, has not attained to the law of righteousness. Why? Because they did not seek it by faith, but as it were, by the works of the law. For they stumbled at that stumbling stone. As it is written: "Behold, I lay in Zion a stumbling stone and rock of offense, And whoever believes on Him will not be put to shame. – Romans 9:30-33*

CAN YOU RECEIVE FROM GOD?

The following story was an enactment from a teaching on how to receive from God.

My friend Leslie brought me a gift basket that was filled with delicious looking grapefruit. She reached her hand in the basket, pulled out the most scrumptious and inviting looking grapefruit, and handed it to me. My job was to say thank you, receive it, and eat it. I did say, "Thank you very much." She said, "I hope you like what's in the basket. I hope you like grapefruit." There, in front of me, was my beautiful gift basket filled with delicious grapefruit.

With my thank you having been said, my next job was to reach out and take the fruit that was being handed to me. I desperately wanted it. My mouth was watering. I could taste it without even having taken my first bite. Leslie was holding it out to me and telling me to take it. I needed it, desperately wanted it, kept asking her to give it to me, was pacing back and forth anxiously waiting for her to put it in my hand, but I never reached my hand out. As much as I thought I was in a receiving mode, without putting forth my hand, I was out of position to receive my heart's desire.

By this time Leslie was practically begging me to just reach out and take the grapefruit. My thoughts were that if I only had one, if there was some way, I mean,

I have wanted one all my life. I began to beg and cry. Would you please, Leslie, would you please give it to me? I don't know. I guess I'm just unworthy. I'm never going to receive it. I'm never going to get it. I don't know what's happening. I'm even going to fast and pray to receive my grapefruit. Everywhere I went I saw grapefruit. Other people have theirs and are enjoying it, but I never get a grapefruit. I have been told that it is mine but as hard as I try to get one, it's just not for me. The thought entered my mind that my mama couldn't get a grapefruit. My daddy couldn't get a grapefruit. Everybody in my family is without grapefruit. I don't know what's going to happen.

Beloved, the blessing of God will chase us down even as we keep believing the lie that we're not worthy, not good enough, or that we haven't done enough to earn the blessing. When people don't receive their blessing, they're quick to think that it's because of something they've done, or failed to do. They are then quick to tell others that they've been left behind because God loves them just the way they are. However, God's way is to love us so much that He does everything He can not to leave us that way. He chases us down only to have us refuse to reach out and take what He has already given. He sees us through His eyes, thinks of us through His thoughts, and only sees us as He sees Himself. He filters every believer through the blood of Jesus. And yet, we cannot bring ourselves to reach out by faith and take what He has already offered as a free gift. He chases us down with healing, deliverance, and prosperity but we keep running from it. We keep running from it because we think we have to do something, walk faster, jump up and down, do more, know more, and be more. We begin to convince ourselves that God's promises are too good for us to take because we're too unworthy and don't deserve it.

God has placed before us the only key we need to apprehend His gifts. We only need to believe. There is nothing hard or complicated about it. The Bible says the religious system wanted to establish their own righteousness by making up endless rules and regulations in an attempt to get what they already had.

Answer the following questions.

But Jesus answered and said to him, "Permit it to be so now, for thus it is fitting for us to fulfill all righteousness." Then he allowed Him. –Matthew 3:15

Why is this Scripture important? Explain.

_____

_____

_____

_____

_____

_____

_____

_____

_____

How is righteousness derived? Explain.

_____

_____

_____

_____

_____

_____

_____

_____

_____

Blessed are those who hunger and thirst for righteousness, For they shall be filled. –Matthew 5:6

What is the condition for being satisfied? Explain.

_____

_____

_____

_____

_____

_____

For I say to you, that unless your righteousness exceeds the righteousness of the scribes and Pharisees, you will by no means enter the kingdom of heaven. – Matthew 5:20

Why are works not sufficient to obtain righteousness? Explain.

_____

_____

_____

_____

_____

_____

_____

_____

But seek first the kingdom of God and His righteousness, and all these things shall be added to you. –Matthew 6:33

What are the "things" that this portion of Scripture references? Explain.

_____

_____

_____

_____

_____

_____

_____

_____

_____

For John came to you in the way of righteousness, and you did not believe him; but tax collectors and harlots believed him; and when you saw it, you did not afterward relent and believe him. –Matthew 21:32

What was the message of John the Baptist? Explain.

_____

_____

_____

_____

_____

_____

_____

_____

_____

Who was interested in knowing how to get the free gift of righteousness? Explain.

_____

_____

_____

_____

_____

_____

_____

_____

In holiness and righteousness before Him all the days of our life. –Luke 1:75

What does this prophetic word mean? Explain.

_____

_____

_____

_____

_____

_____

_____

_____

Study this Scripture and memorize it.

And when He has come, He will convict the world of sin, and of righteousness, and of judgment: of sin, because they do not believe in Me; of righteousness, because I go to My Father and you see Me no more; of judgment, because the ruler of this world is judged. – John 16:8 -11

What are the principle goals of the Holy Spirit? Explain.

_____

_____

_____

_____

_____

_____

_____

_____

_____

Because He has appointed a day on which He will judge the world in righteousness by the Man whom He has ordained. He has given assurance of this to all by raising Him from the dead. –Acts 17:31

Is righteousness extended over all humanity? Explain.

_____

_____

_____

_____

_____

_____

_____

_____

_____

_____

Now as he reasoned about righteousness, self-control, and the judgment to come, Felix was afraid and answered, "Go away for now; when I have a convenient time I will call for you. –Acts 24:25

Why did Paul's message of the free gift of righteousness make Felix fearful? Explain.

_____

_____

_____

_____

_____

_____

_____

For in it the righteousness of God is revealed from faith to faith; as it is written, "The just shall live by faith." – Romans 1:17

Do you believe you are as righteous as Jesus? Explain.

_____

_____

_____

_____

_____

_____

Study this Scripture and memorize it.

But now the righteousness of God apart from the law is revealed, being witnessed by the Law and the Prophets, even the righteousness of God, through faith in Jesus Christ, to all and on all who believe. For there is no difference. –Romans 3:21-22

Is there righteousness available apart from the law or our own efforts? Explain.

_____

_____

_____

_____

_____

_____

Carefully study each of the following Scriptures and relate the reoccurring theme in each of them.

For what does the Scripture say? "Abraham believed God, and it was accounted to him for righteousness." Now to him who works, the wages are not counted as grace but as debt. But to him who does not work but believes on Him who justifies the ungodly, his faith is accounted for righteousness, just as David also describes the blessedness of the man to whom God imputes righteousness apart from works. –Romans 4:3-6

_____

_____

_____

_____

_____

_____

_____

For as he thinks in his heart, so is he."Eat and drink!" he says to you, But his heart is not with you. – Proverbs 23:7

_____

_____

_____

_____

_____

_____

For if by the one man's offense death reigned through the one, much more those who receive abundance of grace and of the gift of righteousness will reign in life through the One, Jesus Christ. Therefore, as through one man's offense judgment came to all men, resulting in condemnation, even so through one Man's righteous act the free gift came to all men, resulting in justification of life. For as by one man's disobedience many were made sinners, so also by one Man's obedience many will be made righteous. – Romans 5:17-19

_____

_____

_____

_____

_____

_____

_____

Did Jesus obey all the law in our place? Explain

_____

_____

_____

_____

_____

_____

_____

Did He give His obedience or righteousness to the redeemed? Explain.

_____

_____

_____

_____

_____

_____

In the year that King Uzziah died, I saw the Lord, high and exalted, seated on a throne; and the train of his robe filled the temple. –Isaiah 6:1, 5

Woe to me!" I cried. "I am ruined! For I am a man of unclean lips, and I live among a people of unclean lips, and my eyes have seen the King, the Lord Almighty. –Isaiah 6:1

When the great prophet said, "I saw the Lord and he was high and lifted up, and his train filled the temple," we know the train is His glory. We understand that redeemed mankind is His temple. He saw something so beautiful, marvelous, and spectacular that his reaction was, "Oh, my God. Oh, my God. I'm a man of unclean lips." He began to look for some way to be able to divert the attention of the grace of God and the righteousness of God away from himself. He said, "Oh, I am a man of unclean lips." Now angels cannot bear to hear unbelief in the presence of God. They just cannot stand it. One of the angels ran over to Isaiah with a live coal that he had taken from the altar of incense and seared the prophet's lips with the coal of fire. Immediately, once the fire of God touched his mouth and he instantly lost the spirit of being unclean, unholy, and unrighteous, he said, "Here am I. Send me. Here am I, send me" (Isaiah 6:6-8).

All unbelief vanished by the fire of God. May the fire of God kindle upon you. There is enough power in your life to renew the face of the earth if you are willing to say, "Here am I. Send me." Begin to confess, "I am the righteousness of God. My life is hidden in Christ. I am who God says that I am." Why do you seek that which you already have? You are as powerful as you are ever going to be but you have to receive it. You can believe that the grapefruit is yours but, until you reach out and take it, nothing happens.

You are righteous. You are holy. You are forgiven.

If the ministry that brought condemnation was glorious, how much more glorious is the ministry that brings righteousness! For what was glorious has no glory now in comparison with the surpassing glory. And if what was transitory came with glory, how much greater is the glory of that which lasts! Therefore, since we have such a hope, we are very bold. We are not like Moses, who would put a veil over his face to prevent the Israelites from seeing the end of what was passing away. But their minds were made dull, for to this day the same veil remains when the old covenant is read. It has not been removed, because only in Christ is it taken away. Even to this day when Moses is read, a veil covers their hearts. But whenever anyone turns to the Lord, the veil is taken away. Now the Lord is the Spirit, and where the Spirit of the Lord is, there is freedom. And we all, who with unveiled faces contemplate the Lord's glory, are being transformed into his image with ever-increasing glory, which comes from the Lord, who is the Spirit. –2 Corinthians 3:9-18

If the ministry of condemnation had glory according to the Old Testament, then the ministry of righteousness exceeds much more in glory. Even what was made glorious had no glory in this respect.

In the Old Testament, the glory of God would visit the prophet, the priest, and the king. It was not an abiding glory in that the law was perfect but had no power. In this respect, the law was like a mule. Do you know what a mule is? A mule is a hybrid burden-bearer. Hybrids are not what we aspire to be. We are, in fact, unique and wonderful. We are the righteousness of God. The law was perfect to reveal to you and me what was on God's mind. You cannot do it, but you can believe it and receive it. Even what was made glorious had no glory in this because of the glory that excels. If what is passing away was glorious, how much more should we expect to receive the gift of glory from the New Testament?

When we see people that are sweating and working so hard to be everything and to do everything, we know that their accomplishments are by the fruits of their own labor. They are the most miserable people. You do not want that for your friends or your family. Everything is bad, and everything is a sin. They are so sin conscious about everything because the power of all sin is in the law. Thank God you are free to love, bring sacrifices of praise, simply receive God's grace, obey, and honor His Word.

> *Do not conform to the pattern of this world, but be transformed by the renewing of your mind. Then you will be able to test and approve what God's will is; his good, pleasing and perfect will. –Romans 12:2*

Beholding as in a mirror the glory of the Lord, we are being transformed into the same image. Whatever you are looking at, that is what you are becoming.

There are things that are going on in the unseen realm of the spirit that are incredibly powerful. It is not about your talents, gifts, or abilities. It is about one believer who will allow the faith of God, not the faith in God, to become activated in them. The faith of God knows and the faith in God hopes.

You have to know there is another dimension. There is another depth of God that takes you away from empty religion and brings you into a viable, passionate relationship with the living God.

> *For He made Him who knew no sin to be sin for us, that we might become the righteousness of God in Him. –2 Corinthians 5:21*

> *Now may he who supplies seed to the sower, and bread for the food, supply and multiply the seed you have sown and increase the fruits of your righteousness. –2 Corinthians 9:10*

What are the fruits of your righteousness that this Scripture verse references?

_____

_____

_____

_____

_____

_____

_____

_____

> *I do not set aside the grace of God, for if righteousness comes through the law, then Christ died in vain. – Galatians 2:21*

We cannot establish our own righteousness for ours is as filthy rags in the sight of God. Only through Jesus Christ, who obeyed the law and gave us as a gift His own righteousness, can righteousness be established.

Just as Abraham believed God, and it was accounted to him for righteousness. –Galatians 3:6

What did Abraham do to obtain righteousness?

_____

_____

_____

_____

_____

_____

Put on the new man which was created according to God in true righteousness and holiness. –Ephesians 4:24

Describe what a new man would look like.

_____

_____

_____

_____

_____

_____

Being filled with the fruits of righteousness which are by Jesus Christ to the glory and the praise of God. – *Philippians 1:11*

In what ways will your life be a demonstration of the fruits of righteousness?

_____

_____

_____

_____

_____

_____

_____

When we begin to believe that we are righteous, we will not be emulators and imitators of what the world is doing but will, instead, be the ones who set the course for fashion, economy, agriculture, education, and the realm of the miraculous to invade the ever-present now.

What is the righteousness of God? Explain.

_____

_____

_____

_____

_____

_____

_____

The righteousness of God is right standing with Him. No matter what I do, even when I fall flat on my face, it does not change the fact that I am righteous.

> *But about the Son he says, Your throne, O God, will last for ever and ever; a scepter of justice will be the scepter of your kingdom. –Hebrews 1:8*

The purpose of a scepter is to render a decision. When Queen Esther made the decision to come before the King, it was a life or death situation. Her mindset was that, 'If I die, I die, but I'm going in before the King. I've come to this point. I have a mission in my mind and now I'm leaving all I know for all I don't know, but I cannot stay where I am and expect to get to another place.'

The scepter is always used to make a decision. The decisions that come from the throne of God are always based on one thing, righteousness. If you are not convinced of your righteousness, then you do not have an entrance to come before the King. You must know that you are righteous.

You might say, "Yeah, but what about the things that I've done and said?" They are under the blood and you are to judge yourself righteous. Do not judge yourself as a sinner. Say, "Father, in the name of Jesus, what I did was not consistent with the nature and the character of God. What I said and what I thought are all behind me. Now, I judge myself righteous. The past has no power over me unless I choose to give it power. With the aid of God's grace, I will go in another direction. I will not walk in condemnation."

If you can get a revelation, an understanding, and a comprehension of the gift of righteousness and right standing with God; if you can begin to understand that, regardless of what you've done, where you've been, or what you've said; if you will judge yourself forgiven and then choose to love yourself; if you will choose to say, "In light of what will last, I don't have a past, I have a now;" if you will choose to act upon the Word of God when it tells you to judge yourself up instead of down; He will grant you the grace to walk in another dimension of truth.

Choose to embrace change.

> *You have loved righteousness and hated lawlessness, therefore, God, your God has anointed you with the oil of gladness more than all your companions.* – *Hebrews 1:9*

Righteousness is the basis for every unction and anointing that will come in your life. The anointing destroys the yoke. The yoke is sin. Sin means you have missed the mark. The anointing of God releases the power of all the promises and provision. The anointing in your life is based on your revelation of your personal righteousness with God.

If you do not know and believe that you are righteous, you

cannot make a withdrawal from what is already yours. You cannot because you are a hope-er, and not a faith-er. You are hoping it is working, but you are not convinced that it is, so your mind has not been transformed; but, it can become transformed if you choose to agree with God.

> Little children, let no one deceive you. He who practices righteousness is righteous, just as He is righteous. –1 John 3:7

The favor of God surrounds the righteous and God declares that He will bless the righteous.

> The eyes of the LORD are on the righteous, And His ears are open to their cry. The face of the LORD is against those who do evil, To cut off the remembrance of them from the earth. The righteous cry out, and the LORD hears, And delivers them out of all their troubles. The LORD is near to those who have a broken heart, And saves such as have a contrite spirit. Many are the afflictions of the righteous, But the LORD delivers him out of them all. He guards all his bones; Not one of them is broken. Evil shall slay the wicked, And those who hate the righteous shall be condemned. –Psalm 34:15-21

Why does the Lord listen to and see the righteous? Explain.

_____

_____

_____

_____

_____

_____

_____

_____

What does He do when the righteous cry out? Explain.

_____

_____

_____

_____

_____

_____

_____

_____

_____

Define the word *cry* in Hebrew. Explain.

_____

_____

_____

_____

_____

_____

Define the word *afflictions* in Hebrew. Explain.

_____

_____

_____

_____

_____

What do you believe is meant by the Scripture, "God liberates the righteous, but evil will slay the wicked?" Explain.

_____

_____

_____

_____

_____

_____

_____

For the arms of the wicked shall be broken, But the LORD upholds the righteous. The LORD knows the days of the upright, And their inheritance shall be forever. They shall not be ashamed in the evil time, And in the days of famine they shall be satisfied. – Psalms 37:17-19

What does the Lord uphold? Explain.

_____

_____

_____

_____

_____

_____

The righteous shall inherit the land, And dwell in it forever. The mouth of the righteous speaks wisdom, And his tongue talks of justice. The law of his God is in his heart; None of his steps shall slide. –Psalms 37:29-31

How do you interpret this verse? Explain.

_____

_____

_____

_____

_____

_____

Read and meditate on the following Scriptures:

But the salvation of the righteous is from the LORD; He is their strength in the time of trouble. –Psalms 37:39

Cast your burden on the LORD, And He shall sustain you; He shall never permit the righteous to be moved. –Psalms 55:22

"All the horns of the wicked I will also cut off, But the horns of the righteous shall be exalted." –Psalms 75:10

The righteous shall flourish like a palm tree, He shall grow like a cedar in Lebanon. –Psalms 92:12

Light is sown for the righteous, And gladness for the upright in heart. –Psalms 97:11

This is the gate of the Lord, Through which the righteous shall enter. –Psalms 118:20

For the scepter of wickedness shall not rest on the land allotted to the righteous, Lest the righteous reach out their hands to iniquity. –Psalms 125:3

The Lord opens the eyes of the blind; The Lord raises those who are bowed down; The Lord loves the righteous. –Psalms 146:8

What is the reoccurring theme in these Scriptures? Explain.

_____

_____

_____

_____

_____

_____

What do these verses say to you personally? Explain.

_____

_____

_____

_____

_____

_____

_____

He stores up sound wisdom for the upright; He is a shield to those who walk uprightly. –Proverbs 2:7

Who has abundant wisdom? Explain.

_____

_____

_____

_____

_____

_____

_____

_____

For the perverse person is an abomination to the LORD, But His secret counsel is with the upright. – Proverbs 3:32

Who gets to hear the secret counsel of God? Explain.

_____

_____

_____

_____

_____

_____

_____

Read and meditate on the following Scriptures:

The lips of the righteous feed many, But fools die for lack of wisdom. –Proverbs 10:21

When the whirlwind passes by, the wicked is no more, But the righteous has an everlasting foundation. – Proverbs 10:25

The righteous will never be removed, But the wicked will not inhabit the earth. –Proverbs 10:30

The righteous is delivered from trouble, And it comes to the wicked instead. –Proverbs 11:8

Though they join forces, the wicked will not go unpunished; But the posterity of the righteous will be delivered. –Proverbs 11:21

He who trusts in his riches will fall, But the righteous will flourish like foliage. –Proverbs 11:28

The fruit of the righteous is a tree of life, And he who wins souls is wise. –Proverbs 11:30

If the righteous will be recompensed on the earth, How much more the ungodly and the sinner. –Proverbs 11:31

The wicked are overthrown and are no more, But the house of the righteous will stand. –Proverbs 12:7

The light of the righteous rejoices, But the lamp of the wicked will be put out. –Proverbs 13:9

Fools mock at sin, But among the upright there is favor. –Proverbs 14:9

The wicked is banished in his wickedness, But the righteous has a refuge in his death. –Proverbs 14:32

In the house of the righteous there is much treasure, But in the revenue of the wicked is trouble. –Proverbs 15:6

The Lord is far from the wicked, But He hears the prayer of the righteous. –Proverbs 15:29

The wicked shall be a ransom for the righteous, And the unfaithful for the upright. –Proverbs 21:18

When the righteous are in authority, the people rejoice; But when a wicked man rules, the people groan. –Proverbs 29:2

Write a paragraph on what you believe is the overall theme.

_____

_____

_____

_____

_____

_____

_____

_____

_____

_____

_____

_____

_____

_____

"Say to the righteous that it shall be well with them, For they shall eat the fruit of their doings. –Isaiah 3:10

If the word of faith is in our mouth, why should we say anything to the righteous? Explain.

_____

_____

_____

_____

_____

_____

_____

But with righteousness He shall judge the poor, And decide with equity for the meek of the earth; He shall strike the earth with the rod of His mouth, And with the breath of His lips He shall slay the wicked. –Isaiah 11:4

How do you think God desires to execute His judgments in the earth?

_____

_____

_____

_____

_____

_____

Blessed are those who hunger and thirst for righteousness, For they shall be filled. –Matthew 5:6

What is the condition for being satisfied and filled? Explain.

_____

_____

_____

_____

_____

_____

_____

_____

_____

Blessed are you when you understand that it is not about your works, it's about what Jesus did if you will just believe.

For I say to you, that unless your righteousness exceeds the righteousness of the scribes and Pharisees, you will by no means enter the kingdom of heaven. –Matthew 5:20

Historians and tradition say that the Pharisees fasted twice a week, prayed every day, and tithed according to the number of seeds in the cucumber. In spite of this, it was still not sufficient. They could not do enough to fulfill the goodness and the righteousness of God.

When the Scripture says seek first the kingdom of God and His righteousness and everything else shall be added to you, it is actually saying God has seen all of our inadequacies, paid the price in total, and counts us righteous simply because we believe and confess that Jesus is the Son of God.

If you have given your life in exchange for His life, confessed that Jesus is your Lord and Savior, died on Calvary as you, and rose from the dead, it is now Christ who lives through you.

Jesus paid a debt He did not owe. I owed a debt I could not pay. The theology is simple. If we seek first the kingdom of God and His righteousness, the entire provision of life that we desire shall be added unto us now and throughout eternity.

> *For John came to you in the way of righteousness, and you did not believe him; but tax collectors and harlots believed him; and when you saw it, you did not afterward relent and believe him. –Matthew 21:32*

The message of John the Baptist is a message of righteousness. He came preaching righteousness, but the religious people that believed it did not want it. They wanted to be able to earn it. It is either a gift or it is a work. Work will not do it. The Scripture says faith without works is a dead thing. You have to have faith before your work is acceptable. If you are working to get something that is a gift, you have frustrated the grace of God and already lost it.

When John came and was proclaiming righteousness, the religious people did not like him. You must understand that religion will not like the message of righteousness because religion wants you to work. Religion wants you working all the time. It wants you to do this and do that when actually you don't have to work, but you get to serve in the Kingdom of God.

> *To grant us that we, being delivered from the hand of our enemies, Might serve Him without fear, In holiness and righteousness before Him all the days of our life.*
> *–Luke 1:74-75*

This is a prophetic word showing that the purpose of God through the death, burial, and resurrection of Jesus Christ was that people would be able to serve God in holiness and in righteousness. Holiness means set aside for the express purpose of God. God has set you aside, consecrated you, and made you holy. You wonder about the times when you have messed up by saying something, thinking something, or doing something that was inappropriate. God already knew all of that and expects you to fall on His mercy.

When you cried unto the Lord and said, "Lord, I did this and Lord, I did that and God, please forgive me for I have sinned." God says He has removed your sin as far as the east is from the west never to be remembered anymore. He calls you righteous, holy, and has paid every debt you owed. You are debt free. Debt free is alive inside of you. It is good to know that.

> *And when He has come, He will convict the world of sin, and of righteousness, and of judgment. –John 16:8*

When the Holy Spirit has come, He will convict the world of sin, not sins. You are going to find out what kind of sin it is. He will convict the world of sin, He will convict the world of righteousness and of the judgment of sin because they did not believe in Him. The work of the Holy Spirit when He has come will convict you, not condemn you. He will convict you and show you that sin does not have any power in your life.

Are you understanding the victory that is ours in Jesus' holy and wonderful name? When the Holy Spirit comes He will convict the world of sin, righteousness, and the judgment of sin. The devil has been judged and defeated. That is what the Holy Ghost comes to tell you. You are not a sinner, you are a saint. You are the righteousness of God in Christ Jesus and the devil is defeated.

One of the principle goals of the Holy Spirit is to convince God's redeemed people that they are just as righteous as Jesus. You are not an imitation of Christ. You are the real deal.

The Word of God is a seed. It goes down into the sole of your soul and begins to germinate. Then that seed begins to grow the crop of righteousness, peace, and joy in the Holy Ghost. Your mind begins to be changed and conformed into the image of the dear Son of God by being transformed through the renewing of your mind.

There is an appointment that God makes with you. That day is the day when you choose to believe that you are righteous. This is the day the Lord has made; let us rejoice and be glad. God will judge the world in righteousness. That means God is going to look at Jesus and call everybody who believes in Jesus righteous, holy, and set aside. He will have erased every trace of condemnation and every sin. Blessed is His holy name!

Now as he reasoned about righteousness, self-control, and the judgment to come, Felix was afraid and answered, "Go away for now; when I have a convenient time I will call for you." –Acts 24:25

Paul is speaking to Felix who is the governor and talking about the free gift of righteousness. He is speaking to Felix and trying to show how God has made us righteous through an inheritance which is a gift.

What do you do to get a gift?

_____

_____

_____

_____

_____

_____

_____

For in it the righteousness of God is revealed from faith to faith; as it is written, "The just shall live by faith. – Romans 1:17

People think they need more faith or that their faith is weak. No. The life you live in this flesh you now live through the faith of the Son of God. The difference between your faith and the faith of God is that the faith of God knows, it does not hope.

But now the righteousness of God apart from the law is revealed, being witnessed by the Law and the Prophets. –Romans 3:21

The righteousness of God through faith in Jesus Christ is to all and on all who believe, for there is no difference. The word of the Lord would have us understand that He has paid the price for all.

For what does the Scripture say? "Abraham believed God, and it was accounted to him for righteousness." –Romans 4:3

What did Abraham do?

_____

_____

_____

_____

_____

_____

_____

You must make a choice to believe that God is in love with you. You have to make a choice to believe that. What does the Scripture say? Abraham believed God and it was accounted to him for righteousness.

But to him who does not work but believes on Him who justifies the ungodly, his faith is accounted for righteousness, just as David also describes the blessedness of the man to whom God imputes righteousness apart from works. –Romans 4:5-6

For as he thinks in his heart, so is he. –Proverbs 23:7

What does that mean to you? Explain.

_____

_____

_____

_____

_____

_____

_____

_____

_____

_____

How is your life a demonstration of righteousness?

_____

_____

_____

_____

_____

_____

_____

_____

_____

_____

For if by the one man's offense death reigned through the one, much more those who receive abundance of grace and of the gift of righteousness will reign in life through the One, Jesus Christ. –Romans 5:17

Jesus obeyed all the law. The Levitical law was perfect. The law reveals to us the nature of God. But the law cannot bring you to perfection. It cannot bring you to maturity.

For He made Him who knew no sin to be sin for us, that we might become the righteousness of God in Him. –2 Corinthians 5:21

Note: When referring to the "Law," we are referring to the Old Testament Levitical law.

Notes

_____

_____

_____

_____

_____

_____

_____

_____

_____

_____

_____

_____

_____

_____

_____

_____

_____

_____

_____

_____

Notes

_____

_____

_____

_____

_____

_____

_____

_____

_____

_____

_____

_____

_____

_____

_____

_____

_____

_____

_____

_____

_____

Notes

_____

_____

_____

_____

_____

_____

_____

_____

_____

_____

_____

_____

_____

_____

_____

_____

_____

_____

_____

_____

_____

_____

About Dr. Clarice Fluitt

Dr. Clarice Fluitt is a powerful international speaker and industry leader. She is a highly sought after personal advisor, author, and life strategist whose message brings inspiration and innovation to every audience she encounters. Dr. Fluitt's insight and delivery have solidified her position as a renowned motivational speaker and transformational voice impacting countless lives daily.

As a global trainer for more than four decades, Dr. Fluitt's success is based on her ability to help organizations thrive for real results. Her experiences as corporate and executive coach, entrepreneur and strategic consultant allow Dr. Fluitt to share her proven strategies for building customer value, creating revolutionary products, inspiring innovation, and generating sustainable growth. She takes the time to understand your organization and your audience, and delivers an informative and highly engaging presentation that will help you and your teams achieve results.

Dr. Fluitt has shared the stage with some of the world's most influential pioneers in the industry to include Steve Forbes, Suze Orman, Larry King, Michael J. Fox, Rudy Giuliani, Les Brown, Daymond John, Rick Belluzzo, Shaquille O'Neal, Joe Montana and many other legendary speakers. Dr. Fluitt's direct approach to transformation is crafted and customized to ensure that every audience is equipped with the tools they need to succeed in today's economy.

More Resources by Dr. Clarice Fluitt

Books
Ridiculous Miracles
The Law of Honor
Inspirational Insights
Thoughts That Make You Think
Developing Your Limitless Potential

For information on Real Results Solutions Coaching
and Mentoring packages:
Visit: www.realresults.solutions

Contact Information
Clarice Fluitt Enterprises, LLC
P O Box 15111
Monroe, LA 71207

Phone: 318.410.9788

E-mail: drclarice@claricefluitt.com

Websites:
www.realresults.solutions

www.claricefluitt.com

Printed in Great Britain
by Amazon

85844180R00041